A HOME FOR US

Written by LaShundra S. Bradley
Illustrated by J.J. Philips and Kai Phillps

I once had a family! A loving family! We used to go to the park, out to eat, have lots of laughs, and do things together.

Then one day things changed! Mom no longer was around. Dad just up and left us one day.

Then it was just me and my sister Pearl.

My sister was the best! She did all that she could to take care of me. She played with me, read to me and she made sure we bathe every night. Sister even tried to cook. Even though it didn't taste so good, I never said a word.

One day there was a knock at the door and my sister told me to never open the door. So we sat and we listened then it went away. The next day there was another knock on the door. I knocked over a glass, so they knew we were inside. This time they had people in uniforms with them. We had no choice but to open the door.

That day at that moment at that time. Our lives changed forever. We did not know what to expect.

All we had were each other.

The lady tried to keep us together, but for some reason that didn't happen. We were separated and left to do the only thing left to do and that was to cry and be silent.

We were able to see each other once a week. Every week it was the same, when it was time to leave we hugged each other and we cried and said "I love you, and we will see you next week."

We begin to see someone once a week and we talk about what went on in our lives. After many sessions we finally warmed up and we found our smile again. We finally started to understand that this may have been the best move yet.

One day my foster parents came to me and said "it's time for you to pack up your things and go to a new home." Oh how sad I was, now this was the third home that I had been removed from.

Why is this happening? What have I done wrong? But little did I know this move would be the last move.

When Ms. Easter picked me up and took me to this colorful looking house, I was very skeptical. But when the door opened I was greeted by the sweetest little lady. I knew everything would be alright.

She said "you must be Korey" and I replied "yes ma'am" with a nod of my head. She said "I have a surprise for you. Do you like surprises?"

I just looked at her with a blank stare. She assured me it would be okay. "Come with me," she said. When I walked into the living room I saw my sister Pearl.

You see Ms. Kat loved children and hers were all grown. She had recently lost her husband and had plenty of room for us. I grabbed my sister's hand and said.....

Finally A Home For Us....

Made in the USA
Columbia, SC
27 February 2022